Moving On

2020

by
Madeline Sharples

Cyberwit.net
HIG 45 Kaushambi Kunj, Kalindipuram
Allahabad - 211011 (U.P.) India
http://www.cyberwit.net
Tel: +(91) 9415091004
E-mail: info@cyberwit.net

Printed at Repro India Limited.

Contents

1. Remnants

Forty Years

He folds her in his arms
and looks down at her
with his deep blue eyes
and a small, closed-mouth smile
that shows just the hint of dimples
in his ruddy cheeks
the way he looked
as he stood at her apartment door
on Mentone Avenue
that first night,
his hair
straw blonde, cut short,
stuck straight up,
his beige raincoat
damp from the March drizzle,
carrying a bottle of champagne
under his arm.

He remembers how
after drinking champagne
after dancing so slow they hardly moved
after she invited him
into her bed
they were up all night
exploring, tasting as they got to know
and feel every inch of each other
stroking faces, necks, thighs, feet,
kissing, mouths open,
almost swallowing each other,

coupling, coming, resting,
one on top, then the other,
spooned, joined
over and over again
until dawn and hunger
drove them out into the rain
to find a place to eat.

And though he admits nothing,
no nothing,
has ever come close
to that first night,
his memory of it
and the girl standing in the doorway
with short dark hair,
a tight-fitting yellow dress,
black patent-leather stiletto pumps,
keep them joined together
now.

Remnants

My father sold upholstery and drapery textiles.
He'd use his shears to cut tapestries,
antique satins, Jacquards, raw silks,
and sheer voiles to size.
He'd call what was left the remnants –
the remainders,
the throw-aways,
the leavings,
all the bits that went into the trash,
gone, forgotten,
making room for the next better piece of material
to come along.

I've been thinking about the remnants of my life,
the little pieces left behind long ago:
childhood girlfriends like Phyllis,
who walked to school with me in first grade,
holding hands, carrying little purses,
and walking on tiptoe,
pretending we were grown up enough to wear high heels,
my favorite uncle killed in a plane crash when I was nine,
leaving me forever longing to tell him goodbye,
getting rid of my baby fat when I was twelve,
falling in love with Eugene
with the gorgeous blue eyes in eighth grade,
who threw me over for a girl he met at camp,
the family house sold and swept clean of old books and toys –
even my first diary with a lock and key – gone,
and my family's move from the Midwest to California
without ever looking back.

Through the years more went by the wayside:
a house in Riverside CA with a view
of orange groves out the kitchen window,
a short work stint on a Pacific island
with my husband and our two little boys,
a job working on proposals
in the aerospace business,
teaching engineers how to write –
and more friends coming and going,
more getting ill and dying
now than ever before.

Also gone are my son Paul and his things:
his old plaid flannel shirts,
Levis with rips in the knees,
Doc Martens worn from his long walks
to escape his demons,
cuttings from his last buzz,
synthesizers,
recording devices,
computer,
records,
and books.
Yet I still have some remnants:
a poem he wrote soon before he died,
a memory of how he looked his last night,
his piano now refinished,
and his room that I turned into my writing room
where he resides as my muse.
These are the remnants I don't throw in the trash.
These are the bits I save.

Intimacy

She moves toward him
her lithe body
her long legs
float across the floor.
Her arms outstretched
wrap around his neck.
And they stop, stare
get to know the color
of each other's eyes.
He turns away slightly
then returns
then turns away again
as if he cannot stand
this closeness
this connection with her.
She leans into him
nuzzles his neck
smiles up into his face
and he relents
and meets her gaze.
He smoothes the length of her arms
and takes her hands in his
and like a dance
they sway
twirl and dip
until almost breathless
their hearts beat together in time.
They lightly hold on to one another
still too new to hang on tight
until the dance is done.

Writing My Truths

I have a new room.
I write in there alone.
I sit at my draftsman table,
looking out the bay window
to the garden.
I see the trunks
of the three palm trees,
the small cement pond,
and the ferns swinging
their leaves behind it.
Sometimes a bird comes
by for a drink,
surfing along the top
of the pool.
Yet, I don't open the window
to hear its song.
I want to hear
the songs my son
once played before he died.
They are my muse.
His memory
lets my soul
listen to the words
in my head. It allows me
to put my fingers
on the keyboard
and write my truths
in silence.

The Lesson

"Worry a little bit every day and in a lifetime you will lose a couple of years. If something is wrong, fix it if you can. But train yourself not to worry. Worry never fixes anything."
Mary Hemingway

If only on that day in July
when she was a chubby tan nine-year old
lazing away the summer
swimming in Lake Michigan,
reading a book curled up
on the red plaid club chair
in her brother's room,
or helping her mom
with her new baby sister,
her favorite uncle,
the handsomest guy she knew,
who said he wanted to marry her
when she grew up and lost her baby fat,
hadn't gotten a migraine headache
and decided to go home to California
one day ahead of schedule.

If only her dad hadn't come home early that day
and stood at the doorway sweating rings
under his arms and telling her mom
in that low clipped voice of his,
"Give me the baby."

If only her mom, hadn't cried out,

"What's the matter?"
as she sat down, squeezing her skirt,
her hands opening and closing
over the flowered print
as it traveled
up and down her thighs.

If only her dad hadn't said,
Phil – that was her uncle's name –
was in a plane crash
in the Burbank mountains,
and was only recognizable
by the ring he always wore
on his pinky finger.

If only her mother hadn't said,
as she ran down the hall to her room,
with her daughter close behind,
"I didn't have time to worry,
that's why it happened,
I was too busy with the baby to worry."

Then she wouldn't have learned
that the way to prevent bad things
from happening is worry
all day and all night, no matter what,
even if a baby has just been born.

Underarm Dingle-Dangle

Semi-inflated balloons
hang under my upper arms.
My friend June used to call this
flapping-in-the-wind phenomena
kimono arms, or, to get right to the point,
underarm dingle-dangle.
They resist every try
to firm them up. I can't bear heavy weights,
and sissy little three-pounders do no good.
Yet I do my puny triceps and biceps moves
at least three times a week anyway.
I've exercised like a fiend
most of my life: playing tennis, running,
practicing Pilates and Yoga,
and now walking miles
along the ocean.
My obsession keeps me sane –
it saved my life and
out of the psych ward after my son died –
and trim enough to defy
those who called me fatso
when I was a little girl.
No, I can't get rid of the dingle-dangle –
I won't it cut off
as once suggested.
Nor will I expose it in public
wearing halter and tank tops
and strapless gowns.
But I can suck it into
a tight-fitting long-sleeved tee.

2. My Jazzman

The Last Night

How could I have known
it would be the last night? A night
like all the others:
the low creaking groan
of the garage door,
tires screeching to maneuver
into the narrow place,
the roar of the engine before silence.
Then slamming the door,
my son, sweeps down the long hall,
calling out hello in his deep friendly voice.
I startle as I hear his heavy strides
pass my door,
I call out to him.
Returning, he enters my room—
standing, staring, looking more calm
than I've ever seen him.
His blue eyes like sapphires
fringed with thick dark lashes
never leave mine while we speak.
My lips kiss his cheek
cool as alabaster.
I marvel at his smile—lips
barely turned up not showing his teeth.
He looks like the angel
he will soon become.
He has already found peace.
Only I don't know it yet.

A Stone Called Son

I sleep with a stone.
It's gray and small enough
to fit in the palm of my hand.
One side is smooth, the other
has the word "son" cut into it.
And when I put the stone
in the crook of my index finger,
I can read the word with my thumb.
I like to place it between my breasts
and feel its coolness on my chest.
It quiets the pain in my heart
and slows down my heartbeats
so I can rest.
Sometimes I hold it all night
and find it in my fist when I wake.
When I'm not sleeping, it sits next to my bed
on a tiny silk pillow imprinted on one side
with the word "heal."
Well, it takes time.
A healing pillow and a stone called son
can't do all the work.

Thursday Morning

When all I heard was silence
behind the locked bathroom door
that Thursday morning,
when all I saw was darkness
through the open bedroom door
when Bob went to investigate,
calling his name, Paul,
pleading with him, Paul,
open the door,
when Bob went to the garage
for a screwdriver to pick the lock,
when he opened the door
and closed it quickly from the inside
while I stood on the stairs,
waiting
as Bob found our son in the bathtub,
sitting in a pool of blood,
blue, already cold and stiff,
tongue hanging out of his mouth,
when Bob came out of the bathroom
face red, hands shaking
and told me
Paul is dead,
when all I heard were sirens
and the footsteps of the police
as they stomped though our house,
all I could do was huddle
in the corner of the couch,
my legs drawn under me,

my arms folded around me,
as I rocked back and forth,
my hands clamped into tight fists.

Making It Hard

The bright room is almost full.
All four walls of mirrors reflect women and men
in baggy shorts and sleek black tights.
The music is so loud
the woman in front of me stuffs earplugs in her ears.
Lisa G says, "work from the core;
your workout relates to your real life."
I want to get on with it.
I don't come here at 6 A.M. to listen to a lecture.
The neon sign on the wall says "sweat,"
and that's what I want to do.
The woman behind me complains.
I don't know her name, but here she is every week
always in the same spot, always complaining, always in black.
Black tights, black sports bra, black thong leotard,
black headband on her head of black hair.
Even her lipstick looks black.
A drill sergeant in baseball cap and high-top aerobic shoes,
Lisa begins her litany.
"If it were easy, everyone would be fit," she shouts,
"Don't come here and expect it to be easy."
She doesn't know my name. I like it that way.
I like the feeling of being anonymous here.
I don't know anyone and no one knows me.
No one knows about Paul, that he died
or any other thing about me either.
Being anonymous is a benefit.
It keeps me in shape, calms my mind,
gives me the space to be myself.

It's a mini-vacation from the horrors of my life.
So I thank Lisa G
for getting me moving,
for making it hard,
for making it hurt,
for showing me how to
trade one pain for another.

The Dreaded Question

It happens again like so many times before.
I'm at my sister's house,
talking to her neighbor,
someone I've just met,
and she asks me the dreaded question,
one that I'm avoiding
by talking about what a great day
this has been in Portland
and isn't my sister's garden just beautiful
and what do you do for a living
and where are you from.
And there it is,
after I've tossed the salad greens
put the tomatoes in the bowl
and sliced in the avocado
"How many children do you have?" she asks.
And never missing a beat
I say, I had two
but now, only one.
My oldest son died.
Then I leave to get myself together
and wonder what she and my sister are saying
while I am lying down in my room.

Aftermath

They came in droves at first,
out of concern, out of curiosity.
They sent flowers, cards
and sweet notes saying
call anytime,
anytime at all.
Now it is quiet.
A few friends
invite us out
or come by.
The rest have moved on,
glad to have done their duty.
They now have nothing left to say.
Don't they know I'm not contagious?
My son's death will not rub off on them.
I'm the same person I was before.
A sadder person, perhaps,
but needing my friends
just the same.

Paul's Tree

It has to be a climbing tree, I say
to replace the one
he used to climb as a boy,
to remind me of him
sitting in the wide Vee
of the upper branches
smiling and proud
of his climbing success.
I settle on a small coral tree
that promises pinky – orange blooms
and strong branches for climbing and sitting,
and place it in its designated spot
exactly one year after his death.
In the thirteen years since,
Paul's tree has produced
dark green leaves –
few coral flowers–
and branches that shoot out
wide and tall from its
four ever-thickening trunks.
When it gets its yearly trim.
I cry, don't take too much away,
but the hackers always do.
Except they can't fix its damage.
The driveway cracked, and
last week plumbers
dug a hole as deep as a grave
that butted against it,
chopping away its roots

to take out a broken pipe.
They shake their heads and say,
It has to go or your troubles will never stop.
I shake my head no.
But I know it's grown too large.
Its roots undermine and its thick
and full branches let no sun shine through.
The day will have to come to replace it
with some red-blooming wispy thing,
and a single miniature trunk that will do
no boy who likes to climb any good.

The 27 Club

I've heard twenty-seven is an age
of compulsion and lack of judgment,
when people don't yet have
a sense of their mortality,
or know that drugs and alcohol
could impact bodily functions.
Young sons especially are at risk.

You didn't know
you would become
an honorary member
of a special club,
created for the many artists
who tell their fans goodbye
at that age.

Its membership includes
greats like Brian Jones
who founded the Rolling Stones,
Hendrix, Joplin, Morrison, Cobain,
and now Amy Winehouse.
You joined the group in 1999.

Could fame get in the way
of smart decisions?
Could creative juices only run
on harmful energy?
Or is it a time of developmental tumult
caused when Saturn returns to the angle

it occupied at the time of birth
oh, those twenty-seven years ago?

Black Bomber

Swaddled in this
black bomber jacket all weekend,
I am safe from the Big Sur chill.
It's too large for me.
And that's okay. It was Paul's.
I bought it for him
years ago at American et Cie on La Brea
before he went crazy
and decided to leave us
way before his time.
I like how it snuggles me,
like he's in there too giving me a hug.
It's the only piece
of his clothing I have left.
I've given away the rest:
his favorite plaid shirts
that smelled of sweat and smoke,
the torn jeans he salvaged
from second-hand stores,
his worn brown Doc Marten oxfords
that took him miles on his manic escapades,
and the tan suede jacket
he had me repair over and over
because he couldn't let it go.
Like this jacket –
I'll never let it go.
It has stains I can't remove
and threads unraveling,
My son is gone.

But this jacket—
try and take it from me.
Just try.

My Jazzman

My jazzman
beat it out
on the mighty eighty-eights,
played those riffs,
tapped his feet
bent his head
down to the keys,
felt those sounds
on his fingertips.
Yeah, he was a hot man
on those eighty-eights.

But all too soon
his bag grew dark.
He went down,
deep down.
My jazzman
played the blues,
lost that spark,
closed the lid.
And, yeah, you got it right,
quit the scene,
laid himself down
in that bone yard
for the big sleep.
Yeah, for the really big sleep.

Buddha

"The dead we can imagine to be anything at all."
Ann Patchett, Bel Canto, HarperCollins Publishers, (2001)

He sits cross-legged in a tree
deep in concentration,
the way he would sit on the floor of his room,
learning against the bed doing homework,
composing music, talking on the phone.
His closed-mouth grin shows
he is pleased to be where he is.
No longer a skinny rail, his cheeks filled out,
his skin clear, his eyes bright.
His tree has everything—soft jazz sounds
flowing from all directions,
deep vees and pillows for sitting and reclining,
the scent of incense and flowers,
branches of books by Miller, Tolstoy, and Dostoevsky,
the music of Davis, Gould, Bach, and Lennon,
and virtual communication to those he loves.
He needs no furniture, no bedding, no clothes, no food.
Those necessities are for worldly beings.
The passing clouds give him comfort,
and the stars light his way.
Heaven takes care of him
as he imagines himself
to be anything at all.

3. Old Age Home

The Last Hope

With flowing dark hair
she ran with light dancer's steps to the tree.
She ran around chanting,
singing in praises,
then bowed, raised her arms,
and brought her palms together
to her heart in respect.
She plucked the round fruit
from its thorny stem
and fell to the earth on her knees,
her homespun skirt swirling and spreading
on the ground.
Tearing the tough outer skin open
long pointed fingernails
pried the crimson seeds
from the yellow rind.
She pushed one shiny seed after the other
into her mouth
and as she chewed the thick red juice
ran down her chin, through her fingers,
and on her bare breasts
leaving her sticky
with the sweet fruit of life.
She ran her tongue
over and over her lips
lapping up every drop of the liquid.
She had longed for a child
for all eternity.
This was her last hope.

Goddesses of Age

The crones – our mothers, grandmothers,
aunts, old friends, and teachers –
walk arm in arm in pairs
each one supporting the other
on the old cobble-stoned streets.
They are squat, stout
with veiny legs and thick ankles,
their bare feet in flat sandals
showing jagged toenails
or clothed in thick hose
and wide oxfords.
Some move slowly
barely able to walk,
clutching each other for support.
They are perfectly coifed.
Their hair short and bleached
hides their age
but not too much.
They wear suits
with skirts always below their knees.
Jeans just don't do.
They talk as they walk
closely together.
Almost in a whisper
they solve the world's problems,
impart their age-old wisdom
or decide what they'll cook for dinner.
They wear their age
as an example.

Softly, simply, elegantly
they are our muse.
They don't hide
but rejoice in their age
They thrive in their togetherness.
That's what counts.
They aren't alone as they walk
They walk together
as we follow behind.

Old Age Home

Easy chairs in a hushed room
hold shrunken bodies
with dozing heads thrown back,
gray skin, sunken cheeks,
and open mouths
that let out an occasional snore.

Grasping a cane with claw-like fingers
a crone struggles to rise,
wobbles, falls back down,
finally up and out,
she takes slow baby steps
as she walks away.

Wearing luncheon's remnants on her blouse
another pushes her walker
from the dining hall.
Her back is humped, hair blue
and bright red lipstick,
bleeds from her lips.

I shudder
and wonder
if I'll have a place someday
on those chairs with my cane or walker
close by to guide me.
I look down at my aging hands.

No, not yet.

Ninety Years Old

So small between crisp white sheets
a tiny head, wispy white hair
hanging in strings around your sagging face
and a mouth that has forgotten how to smile,
you lie crumpled and limp
like a discarded doll.

Your skin shines like fragile rice paper
peppered with brown spots
You reach your red-painted claws out to me
"Please take me home," you cry,
"I can take care of myself."
I have to say, "no."

You sink back deeper into your bed
clutching your knees to your breast.
Filmed over with mist
your vacant eyes only stare.
You don't see or hear me anymore.

Long Division

I gathered all the papers that had piled high
on my desk for weeks and put them
into nice neat stacks – Medicare receipts,
bank statements, insurance policy,
tax stuff, paid bills, unpaid bills, funeral records,
and a special pile called Memorabilia –
with her typed up life story in her own words,
her citizenship decree and
her husband's death certificate.
I shoved the papers into file folders
and put them into the bottom left hand drawer
of my desk. Out of the way, out of sight and
out of mind. This division of papers was the last step.

We had already divided her things.
My brother got the breakfront,
my sister took home the Royal Dalton figurine,
and I have her diamond watch.
Each piece of furniture, silver, china,
and jewelry laid out and chosen
by her three children
until there was nothing left.

4. Star Fishing

Still Life

I walk up behind her.
Her champagne-colored skirt
billows up showing
her matching panties,
and long straight legs
spread wide.
I walk around
to see her face full on
and find a Marilyn
smiling, happy,
her red lips parted,
eyes closed.
She holds her skirt
to keep the wind
from flying it up in front.
as a pleated halter
in the same champagne color
keeps her breasts
exactly in the right place.
This Marilyn,
strong, substantial,
built larger than life,
belies the insecure,
melancholy Marilyn
who left us
over fifty years ago.

Ah, Edna

(With apologies to Edna St. Vincent Millay's "First Fig")

Ah, Edna,
if you only knew
how such a small flame ignites
and strengthens me.
It warms my body
through and through.
It makes me
quote these lovely words
incessantly.
But please, oh, please
my friend, tell me
what the hell
the title means.

Through the Parking Lot, Into the Gym

5:30 am
in the dark, the cold, the rain
lines of cars jockey for the space
yeah, you guessed it
closest to the door.
The huge gray flatbed
always in the compact section
just to piss me off

Inside the gym
blinding light reveals every pore,
frown, furrow,
sleepy eye, yawn, bed head
every drop of sweat,
every added inch
gained chomping on chips,
shoveling in the cookies
pizza pies, McAnythings.

The same folks every day
The same serious folks focus
like racehorses with blinders.

The same folks all lined up
in rows of stairsteppers
rows of treadmills
rows of elliptical trainers
rows of bikes
rows of rowers,

ab crunchers, thigh shavers,
hip slimmers, arm deflabbers, chest expanders,
dumbbells, barbells, bars with no bells
and no whistles.

They're on slant boards, flat boards, balance boards,
wood floors, carpeted floors, balls, bozus
You ask what's a bozu? – it's a half ball.
You have to be there.
You have to try it.
They wear
baggy tees, baggy sweats,
long shorts, short shorts, tight shorts,
skin tights, tight tights,
bra tops, tank tops, see-through tops, no tops –
whoops, did I say that?
Really, they all wear tops.
Guzzling, suckling like babies
their sports drinks
from those ubiquitous plastic nipples.

They're plugged in
to iPhones, iPods, radios, TVs.
Anything to drown out the drone,
the cacophony of weights bouncing off the floor,
feet clip pity clopping on the treadmill,
Anything to miss
the macho guys yelling across the room,
ridiculing, riling up their buddies,
exposing their pecks
and their sex lives.
Anything to erase
the voice of the brunette with glasses

still gloating over Trump's win –
the I told ya sos
and so what?
Others running, climbing, cycling, walking,
flexing, flaunting, strutting their siliconed stuff.
The old geezers checking out the babes.
The comes ons, turn ons, hard ons and on and on.

They're all there when I'm there
every day, every morning
day in, day out.
5:30 am.

Purple Artichokes

I bought four purple artichokes,
round, full, perfect
for our first course.
The color called to me.
I'd seen light purple artichoke blooms,
but these had deep
purple leaves instead of green.
I sawed about two inches
off their tips
with my largest chef's knife,
cut the stems flush with their bottoms,
and packed them tightly
in my biggest pot.
I cooked them as usual.
Water to cover,
a few glugs of olive oil,
a squeeze of half a lemon
before throwing the rest into the pot.
Then with a few grinds of salt and pepper
and a dash of Emeril's bam
I started the boil,
and lowered the flame to a slow simmer
until an hour later
a fork told me they were done.
As I placed them
on our white artichoke plates,
dressed with a little mayo-ketchup mix,
I missed their purpleness.
The finished product turned out
green artichokes
that tasted the same as usual.

Star Fishing

Today I want to tell you about variable stars.
They intrigue me because they change.
They change in brightness.
Some repeat cycles with almost clocklike precision
others change irregularly.
Some require only hours or days
to return to their starting brightness.
Others require years to change.
Yet, whether they change imperceptibly or violently
all variable stars change.

The most spectacular variable is the Nova.
It can get up to 200,000 times brighter than the Sun.
But, alas, it is temporary.
It periodically blows off a tiny percent of the Sun's mass
at speeds up to 600 miles a second
until it loses too much mass to continue.
Whereas Supernovas brighten up to 10 billion times
the Sun's brightness for a few days
and then fade away forever.

One more thing.
Variable stars change their brightness by pulsating
ever expanding and contracting
like a balloon.
They repeat their brightness cycles
from one day to hundreds of days
and are hundreds of times more luminous
than the Sun.

Well, that's it.

Now go out into your yard
lean back in your recliner
gaze up into that black starry sky
and see if you can find your own variable star
amidst the 8000 stars visible to the naked eye.

See if you can catch its luminosity.

Surely you can. Surely you can.

Plucking to Kill Time

So I'm waiting at the stoplight
at the corner of Marine and Sepulveda
and happened to glance over at the car
in the lane to my left.
The car was like my husband's,
a gray Toyota Camry,
but that's where any similarities stopped.
Inside a lady in the driver's seat
busily scrunched her chin
from side to side
and up and down
and contorted her mouth every which way
as she peered into the sunshade mirror
and plucked out her chin hairs.
Her readers hung low on her nose
while her fingers and those tweezers moved
around her chin a mile a minute.
I was fascinated. I couldn't help myself.
I kept looking over until the light changed
and she took off her glasses,
set her tweezers aside,
moved the shade out of her way,
and drove North with the rest of us.

Snapshot

He sits with us at the table,
his stomach bulging
his cheeks puffed out
as he spreads the cream cheese
over the entire surface
of the bagel he holds in his palm.
He sets the bagel down,
piles cucumber, tomato
and onion slices
and smoked salmon on top.
As he bites
a portion falls
onto the red paper napkin he has tucked
into a button hole
high on his chest.
Whew, he is able to salvage it
and shove it into his mouth.

Stop and Go

On the drive up the coast
I pass through Vista del Mar
with the Pacific Ocean
on my left.
This morning it looks like silver glass.
I get on the 405 chugging along
through the construction at Sunset
the Getty, Skirball and the depths of
the San Fernando Valley.
It is alternating stop and go
with bursts of 80 mile an hour straight-aways.
My mind wanders, not paying enough
attention to my audio book,
Mary Coin, about that
iconic Oakie lady,
gaunt and gray,
taking a sit-down
by the side of the road
while photographed
by my favorite Dorothea Lange.
But this is fiction.
No one knows the real Mary,
or even if her name was Mary.
I keep going,
moving my feet about the floor
one pushing down on the pedal
the other pumping in and out
trying to soothe the vague pain
in my left calf.

I press my hands on the ceiling
one after the other
but my car has no room
for a full stretch.
Once I pass Santa Barbara
the hills are vast with mustard,
the sky stormy,
overcast with lingering clouds.
I turn off the radio
relish the silence
of driving alone thinking
about getting to Big Sur,
my calming and writing place
and try to forget last week.
I had a blood clot ruled out.
The same day my husband had
carpel tunnel surgery.
The next, a seven-foot hole
that looked like a grave
was dug in my garden
to replace a broken pipe.
Saturday night I served dinner
for ten friends.
We ate sushi, tzatziki, chicken,
swordfish, and my mother's peach ping recipe
made from this season's sweetest fruit.
We talked about six degrees of separation,
who do you know,
what a small world this is
while I tried desperately
not to think of Cynthia's
recurring cancer,
her sad, scared eyes,

gazing at the white lilies
adorning the table,
her thin body looking thinner yet
in all black,
as I hope someone
somewhere will find
her a miracle cure.

No Helmets Yet

They wear no helmets for this game.
Children, ages nine and ten,
play flag football
under a gray-clouded sky.

No pushing or tackling allowed yet.
Instead, they pull off a belt
of flags from
around their opponent's waists
to end a play.

As we scream for more,
the youngsters pass the football
twenty-five yards or more,
until the team's only girl,
her red blonde ponytail
and feet flying, catches it
and runs for a touchdown.

We buy them footballs to fit
in their small hands,
and entice them with our roars.
Soon we'll add helmets
and shoulder and knee pads
and cheer for them even more
when they knock their heads together,
and heave each other to the ground.

5. Since He Left His Toothbrush

My last chance

For a hug
and the words,
I love you
died with him
as he walked down the hall,
into his dark room,
and forever out of my sight.

Better Off Quiet

Enough stomping and pounding.
Five days is enough.
Fixing a leaky roof
tries the patience of
those underneath
writing twitter poems
and such.

Injury

After eight weeks
he can step down
gingerly at first, until he can walk
without pain or crutch.
The next hurdle
is getting back
behind the wheel.

Riding the Waves

Hummingbirds are skinny-dipping
in my garden pool,
bouncing off the fountain,
surfing the surrounding leaves.

Since He Left His Toothbrush

He recited Byron's words
"yet we'll go no more a roving
by the light of the moon"
as a final fare thee well,
but she knew he'd be back.

Autumn Isolation

I like that as the trees rustle outside,
stripping in the sunlight,
I can't hear their sway
I can't hear their song.

Walk

I walk in morning's dark
before moonset and sunrise
No surfers, one fisherman
on the pier, no waiting
for cars at the light.

6. Demolition

Blizzard in B

It is mid-March,1993,
and a bitter blizzard blows in.
Some predict
the century's biggest.

Flakes of snow swirl in gusts to the sidewalk.
Cold slaps our cheeks
pushes through our clothes
as we cling to each other,
walking through the cavern
at the feet of New York's skyscrapers.
The sirens set our teeth chattering
as impatient cabbies honk,
inch their way up the streets.

Yet, we trudge forward
uncertain of what
we will discover when we arrive.
A more foreboding blizzard, perhaps,
blows through our boy's broken brain.

Mania

Intoxicated, euphoric,
exhilarated, with visions
of power without bounds,
Paul is like Superman.
He climbs, he circles, he races,
he floats above reality
until paranoia removes all
semblance of his sanity.
Then he sees demons lurking in alleyways,
imaginary Mafioso poisoning his drinks and cigarettes
as well as the world's water supply.
He is left to wander, pace,
click door latches as he goes in and out
of the house and up and down the stairs.
While he babbles unintelligibly, imperceptibly,
he keeps time to his internal orchestrations.

The voices he hears echo like violins
ever louder, faster, discordant
until a cacophony of drumbeats
and a tintinnabulation of scraping symbols
pound his brain.
He looks for an exit
where none exists.
There is no escape, no way out
except death
and eternal silence.

The Day My Son Died

[In the style of Frank O'Hara]

It is 7 am in Manhattan Beach a Thursday
three days after Yom Kippur, yes
it is 1999 and I go downstairs to the laundry room
to fold the clothes left there for days
and think about the notice of my ex-father-in-law's
death in the LA Times.

I'm wearing my purple chenille bathrobe
that I've had for years
and I fold for 20 minutes or so
before I realize no noise coming
from behind the closed bathroom door,
the room next to the laundry
where Paul should be, getting ready for work.
                              I go to his room
and the door is half open. I look inside
and it is dark. Then I look in the garage
and it appears he hasn't left yet. His beige Volvo
is still there. I knock on the bathroom door.
No answer.
And I go upstairs.
Bob is just putting on his shoes and socks,
almost ready to leave for work
and I tell him something is not right
downstairs

and he stops what he is doing and
then we go back where I came from to the downstairs
long hall and Bob tries the bathroom door and
yells, Paul, open the door, open the door,
and he goes out to the garage and gets a screwdriver
and opens the door and goes inside
and when he comes out his face,
red with tears streaming down it, says it all.
He tells me Paul is dead, call 911

and I am shaking a lot by now and
leaning on the stair railing
and Bob holds me
while he whispers Paul is dead,
we whisper, our son, Paul is dead.

Paul's Poem

You didn't even touch me, Mother.
I was only down the hall,
sitting against the shower door
in the blue bathtub.
I was cold in there.
Why didn't you touch me?
All you had to do was step inside the bathroom.
I was still there sitting on my box cutter
in just a little puddle of blood.
But I was dressed.
I still had on the clothes that I wore to work -
my white long-sleeved shirt and khakis.
It would have been okay if you came in.
You didn't have to keep the door closed.
I was lonely in there.
You could have come in.

Why didn't you come down to the garage
to kiss me goodbyebefore I left home?
Strangers from the coroner's office put me on a gurney
stuffed me in a plastic bag and took me away.
I didn't want to go,
but they had to make sure I was my murderer
not someone else.
You could have unzipped me down to my neck
and kissed me on the forehead or on my lips.
I wouldn't have minded.
Even though my tongue was sticking out a little
I didn't look too bad.

I know you weren't allowed to visit
during my four days at coroner's office,
but I don't understand why you didn't come
with Dad and Uncle Ken to the mortuary.
That was your last chance,
That was your last chance to see me whole
and you stayed home.
Why did you stay home, Mother?
Oh, sure, Dad probably told you to.
But you could have come anyway
How come, Mother?
I wanted you there with me
before they took me away for good
before they turned me into a bag of ashes.
Were you mad at me, Mother?
Were you mad that I did it?
Were you mad that I killed myself?
Were you frightened to see me dead?
What was it?
You know I had to.
You know I couldn't help myself.
You know the voices made me do it.
I didn't want to.
I didn't want to hurt you,
But I just had to do it.
I just couldn't live anymore in all that pain.
Now I'm okay.
And I know you'll be okay too.
You will someday, Mother.
Mother, someday, you will.

Things in Boxes

He left a black canvas box
filled with his music recordings
next to his bed,
the cassette tapes neatly packed
in order of performance.

And on his closet shelf
we found a cardboard box filled
with little games, cars, toys,
1984 Olympic souvenirs,
and Russian buttons and buckles
his uncle brought back for him.

He fit these favorite things
together like an intricate puzzle,
before he left his body
for us to put in a box
in the ground.

Demolition

Bathroom
We don't have to look into that room anymore
and wonder if spots of blood still remain
on the floors and walls.
We've demolished the scene of the crime.
We will no longer step into that tub and see Paul
in his white long sleeved work shirt
and khaki pants sitting against the shower door
in a bloody puddle.
They've taken it all away.
The old aqua blue tub
The toilet, and sinks.
The faux marble counter
with burn stains from the tiny firecrackers
he set off as a teenager.
The god-awful blue and yellow vinyl flooring is gone.
Sterile white tiles and fixtures
will take their place
in a room with no memories
either of life or death.

Bedroom
Six years later
instead of the dark room
he walked out of for the last time
leaving the door slightly ajar
his bed never slept in
his dirty laundry
slung over his over-stuffed chair,

his paychecks left on the side table
uncashed for weeks,
his pictures and posters meticulously thumbtacked
in perfect rows on the walls
his books and records all lined up
in alphabetical order in his closet
along with his shoes and plaid shirts from second-hand stores,
his keyboard, electronic drums, amplifier,
and his music, each tape labeled and packed
in a canvas bag,
so we could easily choose
a piece to play at his funeral.
Instead, the room now totally bare
except for a new bay window
that looks over the garden
and new shiny hardwood floors.
A writing table and a comfortable sofa
will go in there
with space in the closet
for shelves of poetry books,
files of poems hoping to be published.

Garage
Boxes labeled Paul's fiction A-Z
Paul's jazz records K-O
Paul's rock and roll A-F
stacked where I can see them
as I open the door
park my car every evening
after a long day at work.
On top of the boxes
a pile of dungeons and dragon games
one tarnished brass duck bookend

he got for his Bar Mitzvah,
the purple treasure chest
where he kept his pot,
a cigar box filled with medals and belt buckles
his uncle brought him from Russia.

Leaning against the wall
a roll of drawings
he made in Bellevue's psych ward
each declaring his love for Janet
now married with two children.
A photo of her
with high pointing breasts,
slim waist, flat stomach, and round, firm buttocks
shows her proud, and so ready,
though Paul was not.
He let her go
He let it all go
with one sweep of the knife.

The Bully

Paul is a bully,
always waiting to take over my poems.
I'm writing about my mother
who starved herself last year,
hanging on for weeks in a morphine-induced coma,
using up every bit of energy I had
until she finally died.
And here he comes pushing her aside
to get to the front of the line.
He brags so the whole playground can hear.
"My suicide is bigger.
I used a box cutter; she just stopped eating."
And he's right.
Compared to his death
hers was a bump in the road.
He was my beautiful sick boy,
she, a not-so-nice shriveled old woman
who had wished for death for years.
She'd call me a bad daughter for saying this,
but I don't miss her at all.

Three Cemeteries

On a cool, sunny day in Normandy
the breeze does not disturb
the graves at the American Cemetery.
No matter where you stand,
looking diagonally, horizontally,
or straight back and forth,
each alabaster white grave marker
each chiseled engraving
in perfect precision
and symmetry
as far as the eye can see.
The grass covering the graves
mowed just the right height
a shade of green
from a Technicolor garden.
The surroundings –
a rectangular reflection pool
the curved wall inscribed with the names
of 1,557 Americans missing in action,
the center bronze statue commemorating
the spirit of American youth,
and the Omaha Beach below –
create a restful setting
for the 10,000 allied soldiers
killed in 1943 or 44
during World War II.

On a gray, rainy day
in Prague,

hordes of tourists stroll
through the Jewish cemetery.
Their feet crunch
the brown and yellow leaves
covering the ground.
Housing 800,000 graves –
some over 12 layers deep –
this cemetery, not functional since 1787,
is on the verge of collapse.
The packed gravestones lean
in a hodgepodge of rectangular, square,
and triangular shapes
so old, so worn and broken
the Hebrew or Yiddish markings
are hardly readable.
Just like the Jews
who were forced to live
crammed together in
the Prague ghetto,
these gravestones want
to escape the barriers
that keep the visitors and vandals out.

On a stormy day
in Los Angeles
we drive through the gates
of Hillside Cemetery
and curve around the road
to the back wall
and a small plot
of miniature flat rectangular
gray and black marble gravestones
that lie flush

with the closely cropped grass.
These mark the cremated remains
of fathers, mothers, aunts, uncles,
grandparents.

Full sun interrupts the downpour
just long enough
for us to kneel
at our son's grave
on his December 31st birthday,
wipe away the raindrops,
leave a smooth black stone,
four yellow roses,
and allow our tears to fall.

Tonglen **Practice**

It's the mothers I care about.

When my son died, I grieved for him
and all mothers who ever lost a son.
I breathed in our pain,
And with each exhalation prayed that no mother
would ever have to feel
the pain of such a loss again.

But I can't do it alone.
All mothers over all the world
must do this practice
called *Tonglen* with me.

We must take the pain into our bodies,
into our souls, into our hearts,
and cleanse it with our healing breath.
Then with our collective breathing out
give this world a chance
to be safe for all our sons.

7. Cheetah

A Summer's Day in New York

My back is hot to the touch.
Still, the sun beats down
as the whole world strolls,
taking in the smells at the Union Square market.
Fresh basil, warm bread, cut flowers,
vegetables as vivid as a still life,
all the way from New Jersey farms.
We go to breakfast at The Coffee Shop,
across from the square,
and eat mountains of eggs and crispy fried potatoes
while listening to live jazz.
Afterward, we head uptown on the subway
breathing in the soot, the pee stink,
and body odors
to see the Jackie O exhibit at the Met.
The lines are so long we huddle
against the wall for an hour,
but we don't care a bit.
Then we push and shove our way through the crowds
just to get a glimpse of her clothes.
Over 80 dresses are there - by Givenchy, Cassini and
who knows how many other designers
who made those
60s A-shaped dresses in stiff fabrics
that hit just below her beautiful knees
or skimmed the floors she walked on
with matching coats or capes and little pill box caps
she wore way back on her head.
The sparkly strapless white gown,

its gauzy train
made her look like a fairy princess.
We think of her that way,
mouths open, teary eyed, watching
the clips of her upstaging her husband,
beaming at Nikita, Nehru, or Charles de Gaule,
speaking fluent French and Spanish
as she ignored those rumors about Marilyn.
Those were magical times for both her and me
before our tragedies changed everything.

We leave the Met
walk downtown on Madison Avenue
browsing, trying on dresses,
Jackie O sunglasses,
and shoes until
we can't take another step.
So, we perch ourselves on bar stools,
sip some Chardonnay,
and watch the hordes of people go by.

From Pokerville to Plymouth

Back in the California Gold Rush days
there had to be a place
where those hard-working miners
went to blow off steam.
And Pokerville was it.
Saloons abounded
and pretty girls waited
all gussied up to entertain.
And then the gold rush died.
Yet the town lived on
complete with its hordes of girls
who, all of a sudden
wanted some respect.
They didn't want to be known as
those Pokerville girls anymore.
They campaigned hard,
they marched along Main Street
until the city managers had no choice
but to do away with its infamous moniker.
Instead of Pokerville
the town was henceforth called
Plymouth – a name well-known
for purity – in fact
the epitome of purity.
They couldn't have found a more
pure name in the book.
My only question is:
Where is the rock?

Monet's Lily Pond

Only a few lone blossoms
left upon the pads,
they seem to float
as they flaunt
their crimson and pink petals,
proudly pointing them skyward.
But then an occasional yellow bud
catches the sun's rays
just right,
and we see its
reflection in the pool.

Stonehenge

We drive through farm country
outside of London.
The neatly trimmed fields
have turned yellow
and dry and hot. Huge rolls of hay
lay every few feet
waiting to be picked up
while sheep graze
in the sunlight.

We stop and see
what we came for.
There on barren grass
five-ton stone pillars
built as early as 300 BC
stand at attention.
Other stones just as huge
lay beaten down on the ground.
They say, more stones,
pilfered to use as material
for other ancient structures,
are long gone.

The stones, once used as a calendar
to monitor the summer and winter solstice,
were thought to protect our civilization.
Now, guards must protect them from us.
We cannot get too near
or touch the stone surfaces

so that generations to come will have
their chance to view
this marvel that no one knows
who built or how.

Birches

Sparsely leafed
birches scintillate.
Smooth white barks,
like diamonds,
light up the forest floor.
Their fellow trees
dressed in reds
lime and emerald greens
cannot compete.

That Cat

The gray and tan-striped cat crossed my path
holding a gray mouse in its mouth
almost as big as its head,
distracting me from the poem in my head.
I startled, looked around the corner
as it walked up the hill.
Now I am determined to
blank out that image
of that beautiful little cat,
and forget it could
commit such violence
so foreign to this place and my day,
and think about
the mass of yellow alstroemeria
and pink roses almost as tall as I am,
the browning grass behind the solarium,
the wall of glass around me
that streams in
hot bright light to warm
my always chilly hands
and body and feet,
and how the white waves
seem to float and undulate
as they brush up against the rocks below.
They could lull me to sleep
as I write
like a cat on a full stomach.
But, then that cat,
that beautiful cat sails

back to mind and I'm lost
behind a smoke screen
of serenity.
So why not ask the question,
did that cat like the mouse meal
it had for lunch
or did the proof of its kill
go out with the trash?

Cheetah

The Cheetah sits still
on its haunches in the shelter
of leaves from a fallen tree.
He turns his head back and forth
as his large orange-rimmed yellow eyes
look out for prey.

He shows thin mournful black lines
like tears running down his face.
as he glances toward us.
He does not linger.
We are not what
he wants for supper.

Lions in the Tree

We found four docile lions
in a little dell
high up on the tree -
too relaxed to pay us any heed.
They looked so calm lying there,
like they didn't have
a care in the world.
Or had they just come back
from a kill,
exhausted from tearing
their prey apart,
eating their fill, and leaving
the rest to the vultures.
No wonder they look so content.
They've done their day's work,
and all that is left
is a big long nap.

8. He Just Stopped

Bad News

He's very weak
still sleeping most of the day
caused by low hemoglobin count
and not enough eating.
Today he was taken again
to the hospital emergency room
for infusion of two units of blood
hopefully to help perk him up.
All this bad news leaves me
with constant worry
and scared that he will not survive
this latest setback.
Every time the rehab number
pops up on my phone
my mind immediately thinks
the very worst.

Without Him

I don't know how
I am managing
to walk, to live in this house
to even breathe.
My husband of over fifty years
died last night.
He just stopped breathing
and thinking
and talking
and eating and walking.
He just stopped all the things
that one does to live.
He was done with all that.
He left me alone
to find a way to live without him
to learn to walk again
without him. And I wonder
if I'll ever be able
to do that without him
by my side.

That Last Image

I decided not
to see him dead,
which meant
I couldn't touch him
one last time.
I had seen him
the day before he died
during a FaceTime chat.
He looked wide awake
happy and smiling,
his eyes open
his voice strong.
I didn't want
seeing him dead
to take away
that last image
of him alive
and hearing him say I love you.
Soon I'll have his ashes.
Then I can touch him again.

Cleanup

I've started the cleanup.
Gathering bills
cancelling credit cards
contacting the tax man
and the lawyer
and the mortgage broker.
That is just the beginning.
There are accounts to close
things to donate to charity
other things to give away.
It looks like this job
will take forever
unless I dump it all
into a huge baggie
and put it out for pickup.
But I don't want to do that.
I want to go through
his things piece by piece
and touch each one.

Poem Credits

Forty Years: Leaving the Hall Light On (LTHLO)
Remnants: Porter Gulch Review 2016, Peace Out Poems
The Lesson: The Great American Poetry Show, Volume 3
The Last Night: Memoir (and), LTHLO
A Stone Called Son: LTHLO
Thursday Morning: Memoir (and), LTHLO
Making It Hard – ONTHEBUS, LTHLO
The Dreaded Question: Survivor Chronicles, LTHLO
Aftermath: The Compassionate Friends newsletter, LTHLO
Paul's Tree: Peace Out Poems
Black Bomber: The Great American Poetry Show Volume 1, LTHLO
My Jazzman: Survivor Chronicles, LTHLO, Real Women Write: Sharing Our Stories, Sharing Our Lives 2015 Journal
Buddha: Survivor Chronicles, LTHLO, Peace Out Poems
The Last Hope: The Emerging Goddess
Goddesses of Age: The Emerging Goddess, Story Circle Network (SCN) Journal
I Won't Know Him: SCN Journal
Stop and Go: In the Words of Womyn 2016 Anthology
Riding the Waves: Unfold Magazine
Since He Left His Toothbrush: Unfold Magazine
Autumn Isolation: Unfold Magazine
Walk: @escarp
Blizzard in B: LTHLO
Mania: Survivor Chronicles, LTHLO, Peace Out Poems
Paul's Poem: LTHLO
Things in Boxes: Lucidity
Demolition: Perigee Publication for the Arts, LTHLO

The Bully: Survivors after Suicide newsletter, LTHLO
Three Cemeteries: LTHLO
Tonglen Practice: LTHLO
Lions in the Tree: SCN journal

Made in United States
Orlando, FL
29 September 2023

37374234R00059